PAGAN PAPERS

WALMER BELLES-LETTRES

1. Letters to a Friend *Winifred Holtby*
2. The Letters of Lord Byron
3. Letters to the Sphinx *Oscar Wilde*
4. The Sins of Society and other essays *Ouida*
5. Noted Murder Mysteries *Marie Belloc Lowndes*
6. Pagan Papers *Kenneth Grahame*

GRAHAME on ROADS:

"Some sing you pastorals, fluting low in the hot sun between dusty hedges overlooked by contented cows; past farmsteads where man and beast, living in frank fellowship, learn pleasant and serviceable lessons each of the other; over the full-fed river, lipping the meadow-sweet, and thence on either side through leagues of hay. Or through bending corn they chant the mystical wonderful song of the reaper when the harvest is white to the sickle. But most of them, avoiding classification, keep each his several tender significance: as with one I know, not so far from town, which woos you from the valley by gentle ascent between nut-laden hedges, and ever by some touch of keen fragrance in the air, by some mystery of added softness underfoot — ever a promise of something to come, unguessed, delighting...."

GRAHAME on MARGINS:

"...An authority on practical book-making has stated that 'margin is a matter to be studied'; also that 'to place the print in the centre of the paper is wrong in principle, and to be deprecated.' Now, if it be 'wrong in principle,' let us push that principle to its legitimate conclusion, and 'deprecate' the placing of print on any part of the paper at all. Without actually suggesting this course to any of our living bards, when, I may ask — when shall that true poet arise who, disdaining the trivialities of text, shall give the world a book of verse consisting entirely of margin?.."

GRAHAME on SIN:

"Of pulpiteers and parents it is called Original Sin: a term wherewith they brand whatever frisks and butts with rude goatish horns against accepted maxims and trim theories of education. In the abstract, of course, this fitful stirring of the old yeast is no more sin than a natural craving for a seat on a high stool, for the inscription — now horizontal, and now vertical — of figures, is sin. But the desk-men command a temporary majority: for the short while they shall hold the cards, they have the right to call the game. And so — since we must bow to the storm — let the one thing be labelled Sin, the other Salvation — for a season: ourselves forgetting never that it is all a matter of nomenclature..."

PAGAN
PAPERS

by

KENNETH GRAHAME

SANDNESS
MICHAEL WALMER
2020

Pagan Papers first published 1894 with other essays
First published alone 1898
This edition published 2020

by

Michael Walmer
North House
Melby
Sandness
Shetland ZE2 9PL

ISBN 978-0-6486909-7-6 paperback

Contents

	PAGE
THE ROMANCE OF THE ROAD	9
THE ROMANCE OF THE RAIL	21
NON LIBRI SED LIBERI	31
LOAFING	43
CHEAP KNOWLEDGE	55
THE RURAL PAN	65
MARGINALIA	75
THE ETERNAL WHITHER	85
DEUS TERMINUS	95
OF SMOKING	103
AN AUTUMN ENCOUNTER	115
THE WHITE POPPY	123
A BOHEMIAN IN EXILE	131
JUSTIFIABLE HOMICIDE	147
THE FAIRY WICKET	157
ABOARD THE GALLEY	165
THE LOST CENTAUR	175
ORION	185

THE ROMANCE OF
THE ROAD

Pagan Papers

❦

THE ROMANCE OF THE ROAD

AMONG the many places of magic
visited by Pantagruel and his company during the progress of their famous
voyage, few surpass that island whose
roads did literally "go" to places — "*ou
les chemins cheminent, comme animaulx*" :
and would-be travellers, having inquired
of the road as to its destination, and re-
ceived satisfactory reply, "*se guindans*"
(as the old book hath it — hoisting themselves up on) "*au chemin opportun, sans
aultrement se poiner ou fatiguer, se trou-
voyent au lieu destiné.*"

The best example I know of an approach
to this excellent sort of vitality in roads

is the Ridgeway of the North Berkshire Downs. Join it at Streatley, the point where it crosses the Thames; at once it strikes you out and away from the habitable world in a splendid, purposeful manner, running along the highest ridge of the Downs a broad green ribbon of turf, with but a shade of difference from the neighbouring grass, yet distinct for all that. No villages nor homesteads tempt it aside or modify its course for a yard; should you lose the track where it is blent with the bordering turf or merged in and obliterated by criss-cross paths, you have only to walk straight on, taking heed of no alternative to right or left; and in a minute 'tis with you again — arisen out of the earth as it were. Or, if still not quite assured, lift you your eyes, and there it runs over the brow of the fronting hill. Where a railway crosses it, it disappears indeed — hiding Alpheus-like, from the ignominy of rubble and brick-work; but a little way on it takes up the running again with the same quiet persistence. Out on that almost trackless expanse of billowy Downs such a track is in some sort humanly companionable: it really seems to lead you by the hand.

The "Rudge" is of course an exceptional instance; but indeed this pleasant personality in roads is not entirely fanciful. It exists as a characteristic of the old country road, evolved out of the primitive prehistoric track, developing according to the needs of the land it passes through and serves: with a language, accordingly, and a meaning of its own. Its special services are often told clearly enough; but much else too of the quiet story of the country-side: something of the old tale whereof you learn so little from the printed page. Each is instinct, perhaps, with a separate suggestion. Some

are martial and historic, and by your side
the hurrying feet of the dead raise a
ghostly dust. The name of yon town —
with its Roman or Saxon suffix to British
root — hints at much. Many a strong
man, wanting his *vates sacer*, passed silently
to Hades for that suffix to obtain. The
little rise up yonder on the Downs that
breaks their straight green line against
the sky showed another sight when the sea
of battle surged and beat on its trampled
sides; and the Roman, sore beset, may
have gazed down this very road for relief,
praying for night or the succouring legion.
This child that swings on a gate and peeps
at you from under her sun-bonnet — so may
some girl-ancestress of hers have watched
with beating heart the Wessex levies hurry
along to clash with the heathen and break
them on the down where the ash-trees
grew. And yonder, where the road swings
round under gloomy overgrowth of droop-

ing boughs — is that gleam of water or glitter of lurking spears?

Some sing you pastorals, fluting low in the hot sun between dusty hedges overlooked by contented cows; past farmsteads where man and beast, living in frank fellowship, learn pleasant and serviceable lessons each of the other; over the full-fed river, lipping the meadow-sweet, and thence on either side through leagues of hay. Or through bending corn they chant the mystical wonderful song of the reaper when the harvest is white to the sickle. But most of them, avoiding classification, keep each his several tender significance: as with one I know, not so far from town, which woos you from the valley by gentle ascent between nut-laden hedges, and ever by some touch of keen fragrance in the air, by some mystery of added softness under foot — ever a promise of something to come, unguessed, delighting. Till sud-

denly you are among the pines, their keen
scent strikes you through and through,
their needles carpet the ground, and in
their swaying tops moans the unappeas-
able wind — sad, ceaseless, as the cry of
a warped humanity. Some paces more,
and the promise is fulfilled, the hints and
whisperings become fruition: the ground
breaks steeply away, and you look over
a great inland sea of fields, homesteads,
rolling woodland, and — bounding all,
blent with the horizon, a greyness, a
gleam — the English Channel. A road of
promises, of hinted surprises, following
each other with the inevitable sequence
in a melody.

But we are now in another and stricter
sense an island of *chemins qui cheminent:*
dominated, indeed, by them. By these the
traveller, veritably *se guindans*, may reach
his destination " *sans se poiner ou se fatiguer* " (with large qualifications) ; but **sans**

The Romance of the Road

very much else whereof he were none the worse. The gain seems so obvious that you forget to miss all that lay between the springing stride of the early start and the pleasant weariness of the end approached, when the limbs lag a little as the lights of your destination begin to glimmer through the dusk. All that lay between! "A Day's Ride a Life's Romance" was the excellent title of an unsuccessful book; and indeed the journey should march with the day, beginning and ending with its sun, to be the complete thing, the golden round, required of it. This makes that mind and body fare together, hand in hand, sharing the hope, the action, the fruition; finding equal sweetness in the languor of aching limbs at eve and in the first god-like intoxication of motion with braced muscle in the sun. For walk or ride take the mind over greater distances than a throbbing whirl with stiffening joints and cramped limbs through a dozen counties. Surely you seem to cover vaster spaces with Lavengro, footing it with gipsies or driving his tinker's cart across lonely commons, than with many a globe-trotter or steam-yachtsman with diary or log? And even that dividing line — strictly marked and rarely overstepped — between the man who bicycles and the man who walks, is less due to a prudent regard for personal safety of the one part than to an essential difference in minds.

There is a certain supernal, a deific, state of mind which may indeed be experienced in a minor degree, by any one, in the siesta part of a Turkish bath. But this particular golden glow of the faculties is only felt at its fulness after severe and prolonged exertion in the open air. "A man ought to be seen by the gods," says Marcus Aurelius, "neither dissatisfied with anything, nor complaining." Though this

The Romance of the Road

does not sound at first hearing an excessive demand to make of humanity, yet the gods, I fancy, look long and often for such a sight in these unblest days of hurry. If ever seen at all, 'tis when after many a mile in sun and wind — maybe rain — you reach at last, with the folding star, your destined rustic inn. There, in its homely, comfortable strangeness, after unnumbered chops with country ale, the hard facts of life begin to swim in a golden mist. You are isled from accustomed cares and worries — you are set in a peculiar nook of rest. Then old failures seem partial successes, then old loves come back in their fairest form, but this time with never a shadow of regret, then old jokes renew their youth and flavour. You ask nothing of the gods above, nothing of men below — not even their company. To-morrow you shall begin life again: shall write your book, make your fortune, do anything; meanwhile you sit, and the jolly world swings round, and you seem to hear it circle to the music of the spheres. What pipe was ever thus beatifying in effect? You are aching all over, and enjoying it; and the scent of the limes drifts in through the window. This is undoubtedly the best and greatest country in the world; and none but good fellows abide in it.

> " Laud we the Gods,
> And let our crooked smokes climb to their nostrils
> From our blest altars."

THE ROMANCE OF
THE RAIL

THE ROMANCE OF THE RAIL

IN these iron days of the dominance of steam, the crowning wrong that is wrought us of furnace and piston-rod lies in their annihilation of the steadfast mystery of the horizon, so that the imagination no longer begins to work at the point where vision ceases. In happier times, three hundred years ago, the seafarers from Bristol City looked out from the prows of their vessels in the grey of the morning, and wot not rightly whether the land they saw might be Jerusalem or Madagascar, or if it were not North and South America. "And there be certaine flitting islands," says one, "which have been oftentimes seene, and when men approached near them they vanished."

Pagan Papers

"It may be that the gulfs will wash us down," said Ulysses (thinking of what Americans call the "getting-off place"); "it may be we shall touch the Happy Isles." And so on, and so on; each with his special hope or "wild surmise." There was always a chance of touching the Happy Isles. And in that first fair world whose men and manners we knew through story-books, before experience taught us far other, the Prince mounts his horse one fine morning, and rides all day, and sleeps in a forest; and next morning, lo! a new country: and he rides by fields and granges never visited before, through faces strange to him, to where an unknown King steps down to welcome the mysterious stranger. And he marries the Princess, and dwells content for many a year; till one day he thinks "I will look upon my father's face again, though the leagues be long to my own land."

The Romance of the Rail

And he rides all day, and sleeps in a forest; and next morning he is made welcome at home, where his name has become a dim memory. Which is all as it should be; for, annihilate time and space as you may, a man's stride remains the true standard of distance; an eternal and unalterable scale. The severe horizon, too, repels the thoughts as you gaze to the infinite considerations that lie about, within touch and hail; and the night cometh, when no man can work.

To all these natural bounds and limitations it is good to get back now and again, from a life assisted and smooth by artificialities. Where iron has superseded muscle, the kindly life-blood is apt to throb dull as the measured beat of the steam-engine. But the getting back to them is now a matter of effort, of set purpose, a stepping aside out of our ordinary course; they are no longer unsought

23

influences towards the making of character. So perhaps the time of them has
gone by, here in this second generation
of steam. *Pereunt et imputantur;* they
pass away, and are scored against not us
but our guilty fathers. For ourselves,
our peculiar slate is probably filling fast.
The romance of the steam-engine is yet
to be captured and expressed — not fully
nor worthily, perhaps, until it too is a
vanished regret; though Emerson for one
will not have it so, and maintains and
justifies its right to immediate recognition as poetic material. "For as it is
dislocation and detachment from the life
of God that makes things ugly, the poet,
who re-attaches things to Nature and the
whole — re-attaching even artificial things
and violations of Nature to Nature by a
deeper insight — disposes very easily of
the most disagreeable facts"; so that he
looks upon "the factory village and the

railway" and "sees them fall within the
great Order not less than the bee-hive or
the spider's geometrical web." The poet,
however, seems hard to convince hereof.
Emerson will have it that "Nature loves
the gliding train of cars"; "instead of
which" the poet still goes about the
country singing purling brooks. Painters
have been more flexible and liberal.
Turner saw and did his best to seize the
spirit of the thing, its kinship with the
elements, and to blend furnace-glare and
rush of iron with the storm-shower, the
wind and the thwart-flashing sun-rays,
and to make the whole a single expression
of irresoluble force. And even in a certain work by another and a very different
painter — though I willingly acquit Mr.
Frith of any deliberate romantic intention
— you shall find the element of romance
in the vestiges of the old order still lingering in the first transition period: the

Pagan Papers

coach-shaped railway carriages with lug-
gage piled and corded on top, the red-
coated guard, the little engine tethered
well ahead as if between traces. To
those bred within sight of the sea,
steamers will always partake in somewhat
of the "beauty and mystery of the ships";
above all, if their happy childhood have
lain among the gleaming lochs and sinuous firths of the Western Highlands,
where, twice a week maybe, the strange
visitant crept by headland and bay, a
piece of the busy, mysterious outer world.
For myself, I probably stand alone in
owning to a sentimental weakness for the
night-piercing whistle — judiciously remote, as some men love the skirl of the
pipes. In the days when streets were
less wearily familiar than now, or ever
the golden cord was quite loosed that led
back to relinquished fields and wider
skies, I have lain awake on stifling

The Romance of the Rail

summer nights, thinking of luckier friends
by moor and stream, and listening for the
whistles from certain railway stations,
veritable "horns of Elf-land, faintly
blowing." Then, a ghostly passenger, I
have taken my seat in a phantom train,
and sped up, up, through the map, re-
hearsing the journey bit by bit: through
the furnace-lit Midlands, and on till the
grey glimmer of dawn showed stone walls
in place of hedges, and masses looming
up on either side; till the bright sun
shone upon brown leaping streams and
purple heather, and the clear, sharp
northern air streamed in through the
windows. Return, indeed, was bitter;
Endymion-like, "my first touch of the
earth went nigh to kill": but it was only
to hurry northwards again on the wings
of imagination, from dust and heat to the
dear mountain air. "We are only the
children who might have been," mur-

mured Lamb's dream-babes to him; and
for the sake of those dream-journeys, the
journeys that might have been, I still
hail with a certain affection the call of
the engine in the night: even as I love
sometimes to turn the enchanted pages of
the railway A B C, and pass from one to
the other name reminiscent or suggestive
of joy and freedom, Devonian maybe, or
savouring of Wessex, or bearing me away
to some sequestered reach of the quiet
Thames.

NON LIBRI SED LIBERI

NON LIBRI SED LIBERI

IT will never be clear to the lay mind
why the book-buyer buys books.
That it is not to read them is certain: the
closest inspection always fails to find him
thus engaged. He will talk about them
— all night if you let him — wave his hand
to them, shake his fist at them, shed tears
over them (in the small hours of the
morning); but he will not read them.
Yet it would be rash to infer that he buys
his books without a remote intention of
ever reading them. Most book-lovers
start with the honest resolution that some
day they will "shut down on" this fatal
practice. Then they purpose to themselves to enter into their charmed circle,
and close the gates of Paradise behind

them. Then will they read out of nothing but first editions; every day shall be a debauch in large paper and tall copies; and crushed morocco shall be familiar to their touch as buckram. Meanwhile, though, books continue to flaunt their venal charms; it would be cowardice to shun the fray. In fine, one buys and continues to buy; and the promised Sabbath never comes.

The process of the purchase is always much the same, therein resembling the familiar but inferior passion of love. There is the first sight of the Object, accompanied of a catching of the breath, a trembling in the limbs, loss of appetite, ungovernable desire, and a habit of melancholy in secret places. But once possessed, once toyed with amorously for an hour or two, the Object (as in the inferior passion aforesaid) takes its destined place on the shelf — where it stays. And this

saith the scoffer, is all; but even he does
not fail to remark with a certain awe that
the owner goeth thereafter as one possessing a happy secret and radiating an inner
glow. Moreover, he is insufferably con-
ceited, and his conceit waxeth as his coat,
now condemned to a fresh term of servi-
tude, groweth shabbier. And shabby
though his coat may be, yet will he never
stoop to renew its pristine youth and
gloss by the price of any book. No man
— no human, masculine, natural man —
ever sells a book. Men have been known
in moments of thoughtlessness, or compelled by temporary necessity, to rob, to
equivocate, to do murder, to commit what
they should not, to "wince and relent
and refrain" from what they should: these
things, howbeit regrettable, are common
to humanity, and may happen to any of
us. But amateur bookselling is foul
and unnatural; and it is noteworthy that

our language, so capable of particularity, contains no distinctive name for the crime. Fortunately it is hardly known to exist: the face of the public being set against it as a flint — and the trade giving such wretched prices.

In book-buying you not infrequently condone an extravagance by the reflection that this particular purchase will be a good investment, sordidly considered: that you are not squandering income but sinking capital. But you know all the time that you are lying. Once possessed, books develop a personality: they take on a touch of warm human life that links them in a manner with our kith and kin. *Non Angli sed Angeli* was the comment of a missionary (old style) on the small human duodecimos exposed for sale in the Roman market-place; and many a buyer, when some fair-haired little chattel passed into his possession, must have felt that

Non Libri Sed Liberi

here was something vendible no more.
So of these you may well affirm *Non
libri sed liberi;* children now, adopted
into the circle, they shall be trafficked in
never again.

There is one exception which has sadly
to be made — one class of men, of whom I
would fain, if possible, have avoided men-
tion, who are strangers to any such
scruples. These be Executors — a word
to be strongly accented on the penulti-
mate; for, indeed, they are the common
headsmen of collections, and most of all
do whet their bloody edge for harmless
books. Hoary, famous old collections,
budding young collections, fair virgin
collections of a single author — all go
down before the executor's remorseless
axe. He careth not and he spareth not.
"The iniquity of oblivion blindly scat-
tereth her poppy," and it is chiefly by the
hand of the executor that she doth love to

scatter it. May oblivion be his portion for ever!

Of a truth, the foes of the book-lover are not few. One of the most insidious, because he cometh at first in friendly, helpful guise, is the bookbinder. Not in that he bindeth books — for the fair bind-ing is the final crown and flower of pain-ful achievement — but because he bindeth not: because the weary weeks lapse by and turn to months, and the months to years, and still the binder bindeth not: and the heart grows sick with hope deferred. Each morn the maiden binds her hair, each spring the honeysuckle binds the cottage-porch, each autumn the harvester binds his sheaves, each winter the iron frost binds lake and stream, and still the bookbinder he bindeth not. Then a secret voice whispereth: "Arise, be a man, and slay him! Take him grossly, full of bread, with all his crimes

36

Non Libri Sed Liberi

broad-blown, as flush as May; At gaming, swearing, or about some act That hath no relish of salvation in it!" But when the deed is done, and the floor strewn with fragments of binder — still the books remain unbound. You have made all that horrid mess for nothing, and the weary path has to be trodden over again. As a general rule, the man in the habit of murdering bookbinders, though he performs a distinct service to society, only wastes his own time and takes no personal advantage.

And even supposing that after many days your books return to you in leathern surcoats bravely tricked with gold, you have scarce yet weathered the Cape and sailed into halcyon seas. For these books — well, you kept them many weeks before binding them, that the oleaginous printer's-ink might fully dry before the necessary hammering; you forbore to open the pages, that the autocratic binder might refold the sheets if he pleased; and now that all is over — *consummatum est* — still you cannot properly enjoy the harvest of a quiet mind. For these purple emperors are not to be read in bed, nor during meals, nor on the grass with a pipe on Sundays; and these brief periods are all the whirling times allow you for solid serious reading. Still, after all, you have them; you can at least pulverise your friends with the sight; and what have they to show against them? Probably some miserable score or so of half-bindings, such as lead you scornfully to quote the hackneyed couplet concerning the poor Indian whose untutored mind clothes him before but leaves him bare behind. Let us thank the gods that such things are: that to some of us they give not poverty nor riches but a few good books in whole bindings. Dowered with

Non Libri Sed Liberi

these and (if it be vouchsafed) a cup of
Burgundy that is sound even if it be not
old, we can leave to others the foaming
grape of Eastern France that was vintaged
in '74, and with it the whole range of
shilling shockers, — the Barmecidal feast
of the purposeful novelist — yea, even the
countless series that tell of Eminent
Women and Successful Men.

LOAFING

LOAFING

WHEN the golden Summer has rounded languidly to his close, when Autumn has been carried forth in russet winding-sheet, then all good fellows who look upon holidays as a chief end of life return from moor and stream and begin to take stock of gains and losses. And the wisest, realising that the time of action is over while that of reminiscence has begun, realise too that the one is pregnant with greater pleasures than the other — that action, indeed, is only the means to an end of reflection and appreciation. Wisest of all, the Loafer stands apart supreme. For he, of one mind with the philosopher as to the end, goes straight to it at once; and his happy summer has accordingly been spent in those subjective pleasures of the mind whereof the others, the men of muscle and peeled faces, are only just beginning to taste.

And yet though he may a little despise (or rather pity) them, the Loafer does not dislike nor altogether shun them. Far from it: they are very necessary to him. For "*Suave mari magno*" is the motto of your true Loafer; and it is chiefly by keeping ever in view the struggles and the clamorous jostlings of the unenlightened making holiday that he is able to realise the bliss of his own condition and maintain his self-satisfaction at boiling-point. And so is he never very far away from the track beaten by the hurrying Philistine hoof, but hovers more or less on the edge of it, where, the sole fixed star amidst whirling constellations, he

Loafing

may watch the mad world "glance, and
nod, and hurry by."

There are many such centres of con-
templation along the West Coast of
Scotland. Few places are better loafing-
ground than a pier, with its tranquil
"lucid interval" between steamers, the
ever recurrent throb of paddle-wheel, the
rush and foam of beaten water among
the piles, splash of ropes and rumble of
gangways, and all the attendant hurry and
scurry of the human morrice. Here, *tan-
quam in speculo*, the Loafer as he lounges
may, by attorney as it were, touch gently
every stop in the great organ of the emotions of mortality. Rapture of meeting,
departing woe, love at first sight, disdain,
laughter, indifference — he may experience them all, but attenuated and as if he
saw them in a dream; as if, indeed, he
were Heine's god in dream on a moun-
tain-side. Let the drowsy deity awake

45

and all these puppets, emanations of his dream, will vanish into the nothing whence they came. And these emotions may be renewed each morning; if a fair one sail to-day, be sure that one as fair will land to-morrow. The supply is inexhaustible.

But in the South perhaps the happiest loafing-ground is the gift of Father Thames; for there again the contrast of violent action, with its blisters, perspiration, and the like, throws into fine relief the bliss of "quietism." I know one little village in the upper reaches where loafing may be pushed to high perfection. Here the early hours of the morning are vexed by the voices of boaters making their way down the little street to the river. The most of them go staggering under hampers, bundles of waterproofs, and so forth. Their voices are clamant of feats to be accomplished: they will

Loafing

row, they will punt, they will paddle, till they weary out the sun. All this the Loafer hears through the open door of his cottage, where in his shirt-sleeves he is dallying with his bacon, as a gentleman should. He is the only one who has had a comfortable breakfast — and he knows it. Later he will issue forth and stroll down in their track to the bridge. The last of these Argonauts is pulling lustily forth; the river is dotted with evanishing blazers. Upon all these lunatics a pitiless Phœbus shines triumphant. The Loafer sees the last of them off the stage, turns his back on it, and seeks the shady side of the street.

A holy calm possesses the village now; the foreign element has passed away with shouting and waving of banners, and its natural life of somnolency is in evidence at last. And first, as a true Loafer should, let him respectfully greet each

several village dog. *Arcades ambo* —
loafers likewise — they lie there in the
warm dust, each outside his own door,
ready to return the smallest courtesy.
Their own lords and masters are not given
to the exchange of compliments nor to
greetings in the market-place. The dog
is generally the better gentleman, and he
is aware of it; and he duly appreciates
the Loafer, who is not too proud to pause
a moment, change the news, and pass the
time of day. He will mark his sense of
this attention by rising from his dust-
divan and accompanying his caller some
steps on his way. But he will stop short
of his neighbour's dust-patch; for the
morning is really too hot for a shindy.
So, by easy stages (the street is not a
long one: six dogs will see it out), the
Loafer quits the village; and now the
world is before him. Shall he sit on a
gate and smoke? or lie on the grass and

Loafing

smoke? or smoke aimlessly and at large
along the road? Such a choice of happiness is distracting; but perhaps the last
course is the best — as needing the least
mental effort of selection. Hardly, however, has he fairly started his first day-
dream when the snappish "ting" of a
bellkin recalls him to realities. By comes
the bicyclist: dusty, sweating, a piteous
thing to look upon. But the irritation
of the strepitant metal has jarred the
Loafer's always exquisite nerves: he
is fain to climb a gate and make his
way towards solitude and the breezy
downs.

Up here all vestiges of a sordid humanity disappear. The Loafer is alone with
the south-west wind and the blue sky.
Only a carolling of larks and a tinkling
from distant flocks break the brooding
noonday stillness; above, the wind-hover
hangs motionless, a black dot on the blue.

Pagan Papers

Prone on his back on the springy turf, gazing up into the sky, his fleshy integument seems to drop away, and the spirit ranges at will among the tranquil clouds. This way Nirvana nearest lies. Earth no longer obtrudes herself; possibly somewhere a thousand miles or so below him the thing still "spins like a fretful midge." The Loafer knows not nor cares. His is now an astral body, and through golden spaces of imagination his soul is winging her untrammelled flight. And there he really might remain for ever, but that his vagrom spirit is called back to earth by a gentle but resistless, very human summons, — a gradual, consuming, Pantagruelian, god-like, thirst: a thirst to thank Heaven on. So, with a sigh half of regret, half of anticipation, he bends his solitary steps towards the nearest inn. Tobacco for one is good; to commune with oneself and be still is

Loafing

truest wisdom; but beer is a thing of
deity — beer is divine.

Later the Loafer may decently make
some concession to popular taste by stroll-
ing down to the river and getting out his
boat. With one paddle out he will drift
down the stream: just brushing the
flowering rush and the meadow-sweet and
taking in as peculiar gifts the varied
sweets of even. The loosestrife is his,
and the arrow-head: his the distant moan
of the weir; his are the glories, amber
and scarlet and silver, of the sunset-
haunted surface. By-and-by the boaters
will pass him homeward-bound. All are
blistered and sore: his withers are un-
wrung. Most are too tired and hungry to
see the sunset glories; no corporeal pangs
clog his *æsthesis* — his perceptive faculty.
Some have quarrelled in the day and are
no longer on speaking terms; he is at
peace with himself and with the whole

world.   Of all that lay them down in the
little village that night, his sleep will be
the surest and the sweetest. For not
even the blacksmith himself will have
better claim to have earned a night's
repose.

CHEAP KNOWLEDGE

CHEAP KNOWLEDGE

WHEN at times it happens to me that I 'gin to be aweary of the sun, and to find the fair apple of life dust and ashes at the core — just because, perhaps, I can't afford Melampus Brown's last volume of poems in large paper, but must perforce condescend upon the two-and-sixpenny edition for the million — then I bring myself to a right temper by recalling to memory a sight which now and again in old days would touch the heart of me to a happier pulsation. In the long, dark winter evenings, outside some shop window whose gaslight flared brightest into the chilly street, I would see some lad — sometimes even a girl —

book in hand, heedless of cold and wet,
of aching limbs and straining eyes, careless of jostling passers-by, of rattle and
turmoil behind them and about, their
happy spirits far in an enchanted world:
till the ruthless shopman turned out the
gas and brought them rudely back to the
bitter reality of cramped legs and numbed
fingers. "My brother!" or "My sister!"
I would cry inwardly, feeling the link
that bound us together. They possessed,
for the hour, the two gifts most precious
to the student — light and solitude: the
true solitude of the roaring street.

Somehow this vision rarely greets me
now. Probably the Free Libraries have
supplanted the flickering shop-lights;
and every lad and lass can enter and call
for Miss Braddon and batten thereon "in
luxury's sofa-lap of leather"; and of
course this boon is appreciated and
profited by, and we shall see the divine

Cheap Knowledge

results in a year or two. And yet sometimes, like the dear old Baron in the
"Red Lamp," "I wonder?"

For myself, public libraries possess a
special horror, as of lonely wastes and
dragon-haunted fens. The stillness and
the heavy air, the feeling of restriction
and surveillance, the mute presence of
these other readers, "all silent and all
damned," combine to set up a nervous
irritation fatal to quiet study. Had I to
choose, I would prefer the windy street.
And possibly others have found that the
removal of checks and obstacles makes
the path which leads to the divine moun-
tain-tops less tempting, now that it is
less rugged. So full of human nature are
we all — still — despite the Radical mis-
sionaries that labour in the vineyard.
Before the National Gallery was extended
and rearranged, there was a little "St.
Catherine" by Pinturicchio that possessed

my undivided affections. In those days she hung near the floor, so that those who would worship must grovel; and little I grudged it. Whenever I found myself near Trafalgar Square with five minutes to spare I used to turn in and sit on the floor before the object of my love, till gently but firmly replaced on my legs by the attendant. She hangs on the line now, in the grand new room; but I never go to see her. Somehow she is not my "St. Catherine" of old. Doubtless Free Libraries affect many students in the same way: on the same principle as that now generally accepted — that it is the restrictions placed on vice by our social code which make its pursuit so peculiarly agreeable.

But even when the element of human nature has been fully allowed for, it remains a question whether the type of mind that a generation or two of Free

Cheap Knowledge

Libraries will evolve is or is not the one
that the world most desiderates; and
whether the spare reading and consequent
fertile thinking necessitated by the old,
or gas-lamp, style is not productive of
sounder results. The cloyed and con-
gested mind resulting from the free run of
these grocers' shops to omnivorous appe-
tites (and all young readers are omnivorous) bids fair to produce a race of literary
resurrection-men: a result from which we
may well pray to be spared. Of all forms
of lettered effusiveness that which exploits
the original work of others and professes
to supply us with right opinions thereanent
is the least wanted. And whether he
take to literary expression by pen or only
wag the tongue of him, the grocer's boy
of letters is sure to prove a prodigious
bore. The Free Library, if it be fulfill-
ing the programme of its advocates, is
breeding such as he by scores.

Pagan Papers

But after all there is balm in Gilead; and much joy and consolation may be drawn from the sorrowful official reports, by which it would appear that the patrons of these libraries are confining their reading, with a charming unanimity, exclusively to novels. And indeed they cannot do better; there is no more blessed thing on earth than a good novel, not the least merit of which is that it induces a state of passive, unconscious enjoyment, and never frenzies the reader to go out and put the world right. Next to fairy tales — the original world-fiction — our modern novels may be ranked as our most precious possessions; and so it has come to pass that I shall now cheerfully pay my five shillings, or ten shillings, or whatever it may shortly be, in the pound towards the Free Library: convinced at last that the money is not wasted in training exponents of the subjectivity of this writer and the

Cheap Knowledge

objectivity of that, nor in developing fresh imitators of dead discredited styles, but is righteously devoted to the support of wholesome, honest, unpretending novel-reading.

THE RURAL PAN

THE RURAL PAN

(AN APRIL ESSAY)

THROUGH shady Throgmorton Street
and about the vale of Cheapside
the restless Mercury is flitting, with furtive eye and voice a little hoarse from
bidding in the market. Further west,
down classic Piccadilly, moves the young
Apollo, the lord of the unerring (satin)
bow; and nothing meaner than a frock-
coat shall in these latter years float round
his perfect limbs. But remote in other
haunts than these the rural Pan is hiding, and piping the low, sweet strain that
reaches only the ears of a chosen few.
And now that the year wearily turns and
stretches herself before the perfect waking, the god emboldened begins to blow
a clearer note.

Pagan Papers

When the waking comes at last, and
Summer is abroad, these deities will
abroad too, each as his several attributes
move him.   Who is this that flieth up the
reaches of the Thames in steam-launch
hired for the day? Mercury is out —
some dozen or fifteen strong.   The flower-
gemmed banks crumble and slide down
under the wash of his rampant screw; his
wake is marked by a line of lobster-claws,
gold-necked bottles, and fragments of
veal-pie.   Resplendent in blazer, he may
even be seen to embrace the slim-waisted
nymph, haunter of green (room) shades,
in the full gaze of the shocked and scan-
dalised sun.   Apollo meantime reposeth,
passively beautiful, on the lawn of the
Guards' Club at Maidenhead. Here, O
Apollo, are haunts meet for thee. A
deity subjectively inclined, he is neither
objective nor, it must be said for him, at
all objectionable, like them of Mercury.

The Rural Pan

Meanwhile, nor launches nor lawns tempt him that pursueth the rural Pan. In the hushed recesses of Hurley backwater, where the canoe may be paddled almost under the tumbling comb of the weir, he is to be looked for; there the god pipes with freest abandonment. Or under the great shadow of Streatley Hill, "annihilating all that's made to a green thought in a green shade"; or better yet, pushing an explorer's prow up the remote untravelled Thame, till Dorchester's stately roof broods over the quiet fields. In solitudes such as these Pan sits and dabbles, and all the air is full of the music of his piping. Southwards, again, on the pleasant Surrey downs there is shouting and jostling; dust that is drouthy and language that is sultry. Thither comes the young Apollo, calmly confident as ever; and he meeteth certain Mercuries of the baser sort, who do him obeisance, call him captain and lord, and then proceed to skin him from head to foot as thoroughly as the god himself flayed Marsyas in days of yore, at a certain Spring Meeting in Phrygia: a good instance of Time's revenges. And yet Apollo returns to town and swears he has had a grand day. He does so every year. Out of hearing of all the clamour, the rural Pan may be found stretched on Ranmore Common, loitering under Abinger pines, or prone by the secluded stream of the sinuous Mole, abounding in friendly greetings for his foster-brothers the dabchick and water-rat.

For a holiday, Mercury loveth the Pullman Express, and a short hour with a society paper; anon, brown boots on the pier, and the pleasant combination of Métropole and Monopole. Apollo for his part will urge the horses of the Sun: and, if he leaveth the society weekly to

The Rural Pan

Mercury, yet he loveth well the Magazine. From which ὀμφαλός or hub of the universe he will direct his shining team even to the far Hesperides of Richmond or of Windsor. Both iron road and level highway are shunned by the rural Pan, who chooses rather to foot it along the sheep track on the limitless downs or the thwart-leading footpath through copse and spinney, not without pleasant fellowship with feather and fur. Nor does it follow from all this that the god is unsocial. Albeit shy of the company of his more showy brother-deities, he loveth the more unpretentious humankind, especially them that are *adscripti glebæ*, addicted to the kindly soil and to the working thereof: perfect in no way, only simple, cheery sinners. For he is only half a god after all, and the red earth in him is strong. When the pelting storm drives the wayfarers to the sheltering inn, among the little group on bench and settle Pan has been known to appear at times, in homely guise of hedger-and-ditcher or weather-beaten shepherd from the downs. Strange lore and quaint fancy he will then impart, in the musical Wessex or Mercian he has learned to speak so naturally; though it may not be till many a mile away that you begin to suspect that you have unwittingly talked with him who chased the flying Syrinx in Arcady and turned the tide of fight at Marathon.

Yes: to-day the iron horse has searched the country through — east and west, north and south — bringing with it Commercialism, whose god is Jerry, and who studs the hills with stucco and garrotes the streams with the girder. Bringing, too, into every nook and corner fashion and chatter, the tailor-made gown and the eye-glass. Happily a great part is still spared — how great these others fortunately do

The Rural Pan

not know — in which the rural Pan and
his following may hide their heads for yet
a little longer, until the growing tyranny
has invaded the last common, spinney,
and sheep-down, and driven the kindly
god, the well-wisher to man — whither?

MARGINALIA

MARGINALIA

A MERICAN HUNT, in his suggestive "Talks about Art," demands
that the child shall be encouraged — or
rather permitted, for the natural child
needs little encouragement — to draw
when- and whereon-soever he can; for,
says he, the child's scribbling on the margin of his school-books is really worth
more to him than all he gets out of them,
and indeed, "to him the margin is the
best part of all books, and he finds in it
the soothing influence of a clear sky in
a landscape." Doubtless Sir Benjamin
Backbite, though his was not an artist
soul, had some dim feeling of this mighty
truth when he spoke of that new quarto of
his, in which "a neat rivulet of text shall

Pagan Papers

meander through a meadow of margin":
boldly granting the margin to be of superior importance to the print.   This metaphor is pleasantly expanded in Burton's
"Bookhunter": wherein you read of certain folios with "their majestic stream
of central print overflowing into rivulets
of marginal notes, *sedgy with citations.*"
But the good Doctor leaves the main
stream for a backwater of error in inferring that the chief use of margins is to be
a parading-ground for notes and citations.
As if they had not absolute value in themselves, nor served a finer end!   In truth,
Hunt's child was vastly the wiser man.

For myself, my own early margins
chiefly served to note, cite, and illustrate
the habits of crocodiles.   Along the lower
or "tail" edge, the saurian, splendidly serrated as to his back, arose out of old Nile;
up one side negroes, swart as sucked
lead-pencil could limn them, let fall their

Marginalia

nerveless spears; up the other, monkeys, gibbering with terror, swarmed hastily up palm-trees — a plant to the untutored hand of easier outline than (say) your British oak. Meanwhile, all over the unregarded text Balbus slew Caius on the most inadequate provocation, or Hannibal pursued his victorious career, while Roman generals delivered ornate set speeches prior to receiving the usual satisfactory licking. Fabius, Hasdrubal — all alike were pallid shades with faint, thin voices powerless to pierce the distance. The margins of Cocytus doubtless knew them: mine were dedicated to the more attractive flesh and blood of animal life, the varied phases of the tropic forest. Or, in more practical mood, I would stoop to render certain facts recorded in the text. To these digressions I probably owe what little education I possess. For example, there was one sentence in our Roman history: "By this single battle of Magnesia, Antiochus the Great lost all his conquests in Asia Minor." Serious historians really should not thus forget themselves. 'Twas so easy, by a touch of the pen, to transform "battle" into "bottle"; for "conquests" one could substitute a word for which not even Macaulay's school-boy were at a loss; and the result, depicted with rude vigour in his margin, fixed the name of at least one ancient fight on the illustrator's memory. But this plodding and material art had small charm for me: to whom the happy margin was a "clear sky" ever through which I could sail away at will to more gracious worlds. I was duly qualified by a painfully acquired ignorance of dead languages cautiously to approach my own; and 'twas no better. Along Milton's margins the Gryphon must needs pursue the Arimaspian — what a chance, that Arimaspian, for the imaginative pen-

Marginalia

cil! And so it has come about that, while
Milton periods are mostly effaced from
memory by the sponge of Time, I can still
see that vengeful Gryphon, cousin-german
to the gentle beast that danced the Lobster
Quadrille by a certain shore.

It is by no means insisted upon that the
chief end and use of margins is for pic-
torial illustration, nor yet for furtive
games of oughts and crosses, nor (in the
case of hymn-books) for amorous missives
scrawled against the canticle for the day,
to be passed over into an adjacent pew: as
used, alas! to happen in days when one
was young and godless, and went to
church. Nor, again, are the margins of
certain poets entrusted to man for the
composing thereon of infinitely superior
rhymes on the subjects themselves have
maltreated: a depraved habit, akin to
scalping. What has never been properly
recognised is the absolute value of the

margin itself — a value frequently superior to its enclosure. In poetry the popular taste demands its margin, and takes care to get it in "the little verses wot they puts inside the crackers." The special popularity, indeed, of lyric as opposed to epic verse is due to this habit of feeling. A good example may be found in the work of Mr. Swinburne: the latter is the better poetry, the earlier remains the more popular — because of its eloquence of margin. Mr. Tupper might long ago have sat with laureate brow but for his neglect of this first principle. The song of Sigurd, our one epic of the century, is pitiably unmargined, and so has never won the full meed of glory it deserves; while the ingenious gentleman who wrote "Beowulf," our other English epic, grasped the great fact from the first, so that his work is much the more popular of the two. The moral is evident. An

Marginalia

authority on practical book-making has stated that "margin is a matter to be studied"; also that "to place the print in the centre of the paper is wrong in principle, and to be deprecated." Now, if it be "wrong in principle," let us push that principle to its legitimate conclusion, and "deprecate" the placing of print on any part of the paper at all. Without actually suggesting this course to any of our living bards, when, I may ask — when shall that true poet arise who, disdaining the trivialities of text, shall give the world a book of verse consisting entirely of margin? How we shall shove and jostle for large paper copies!

THE ETERNAL
WHITHER

THE ETERNAL WHITHER

THERE was once an old cashier in some ancient City establishment, whose practice was to spend his yearly holiday in relieving some turnpike-man at his post, and performing all the duties appertaining thereunto. This was vulgarly taken to be an instance of mere mill-horse enslavement to his groove — the reception of payments; and it was spoken of both in mockery of all mill-horses and for the due admonishment of others. And yet that clerk had discovered for himself an unique method of seeing Life at its best, the flowing, hurrying, travelling, marketing Life of the Highway; the life of bagman and cart, of tinker, and pig-dealer, and all cheery creatures that drink and chaffer together in the sun. He belonged, above all, to the scanty class of clear-seeing persons who know both what they are good for and what they really want. To know what you would like to do is one thing; to go out boldly and do it is another — and a rarer; and the sterile fields about Hell-Gate are strewn with the corpses of those who would an if they could.

To be sure, being bent on the relaxation most congenial to one's soul, it is possible to push one's disregard for convention too far: as is seen in the case of another, though of an earlier generation, in the same establishment. In his office there was the customary "attendance-book," wherein the clerks were expected to sign each day. Here his name one morning ceases abruptly from appearing; he signs, indeed, no more. Instead of signature you find, a little later, writ in

The Eternal Whither

careful commercial hand, this entry:
"Mr. —— did not attend at his office
to-day, having been hanged at eight
o'clock in the morning for horse-steal-
ing." Through the faded ink of this
record do you not seem to catch, across
the gulf of years, some waft of the jolly
humanity which breathed in this prince
among clerks? A formal precisian, doubtless, during business hours; but with just
this honest love of horseflesh lurking deep
down there in him — unsuspected, sweet-
ening the whole lump. Can you not behold him, freed from his desk, turning to
pursue his natural bent, as a city-bred dog
still striveth to bury his bone deep in the
hearth-rug? For no filthy lucre, you may
be sure, but from sheer love of the pursuit
itself! All the same, he erred; erred, if
not in taste, at least in judgment: for we
cannot entirely acquit him of blame for
letting himself be caught.

Pagan Papers

In these tame and tedious days of the
policeman rampant, our melancholy selves
are debarred from many a sport, joyous
and debonair, whereof our happier fathers
were free. Book-stealing, to be sure, remains to us; but every one is not a col-
lector; and, besides, 'tis a diversion you
can follow with equal success all the year
round. Still, the instance may haply be
pregnant with suggestion to many who
wearily ask each year, what new place or
pursuit exhausted earth still keeps for the
holiday-maker. 'Tis a sad but sober fact,
that the most of men lead flat and virtuous lives, departing annually with their
family to some flat and virtuous place,
there to disport themselves in a manner
that is decent, orderly, wholly uninterest-
ing, vacant of every buxom stimulus. To
such as these a suggestion, in all friend-
liness: why not try crime? We shall not
attempt to specify the particular branch

The Eternal Whither

— for every one must himself seek out and find the path his nature best fits him to follow; but the general charm of the prospect must be evident to all. The freshness and novelty of secrecy, the artistic satisfaction in doing the act of self-expression as well as it can possibly be done; the experience of being not the hunter, but the hunted, not the sportsman, but the game; the delight of comparing and discussing crimes with your mates over a quiet pipe on your return to town; these new pleasures — these and their like — would furnish just that gentle stimulant, that peaceful sense of change so necessary to the tired worker. And then the fact, that you would naturally have to select and plan out your particular line of diversion without advice or assistance, has its own advantage. For the moment a man takes to dinning in your ears that you ought, you really ought, to go to

Pagan Papers

Norway, you at once begin to hate Norway
with a hate that ever will be; and to have
Newlyn, Cromer, or Dawlish, Carinthia
or the Austrian Tyrol jammed down your
throat, is enough to initiate the discovery
that your own individual weakness is a
joyous and persistent liking for man-
slaughter.

Some few seem to be born without much
innate tendency to crime.   After all, it is
mostly a matter of heredity; these unfor-
tunates are less culpable than their neglect-
ful ancestors; and it is a fault that none
need really blush for in the present.   For
such as they there still remains the
example of the turnpike-loving clerk, with
all its golden possibilities.   Denied the
great delight of driving a locomotive, or
a fire-engine — whirled along in a glorious
nimbus of smoke-pant, spark-shower, and
hoarse warning roar — what bliss to the
palefaced quilldriver to command a penny

The Eternal Whither

steamboat between London Bridge and
Chelsea! to drive a four-horsed Jersey-car
to Kew at sixpence a head! Though turn-
pikes be things of the past, there are still
tolls to be taken on many a pleasant reach
of Thames. What happiness in quiet moments to tend the lock-keeper's flower-
beds — perhaps make love to his daughter;
anon in busier times to let the old gates
swing, work the groaning winches, and
hear the water lap and suck and gurgle as
it slowly sinks or rises with its swaying
freight; to dangle legs over the side and
greet old acquaintances here and there
among the parti-coloured wayfarers pass-
ing up or down; while tobacco palleth not
on the longest day, and beer is ever within
easy reach. The iron tetter that scurfs
the face of our island has killed out the
pleasant life of the road; but many of its
best conditions still linger round these
old toll-gates, free from dust and clatter,

on the silent liquid Highway to the West.

These for the weaker brethren: but for him who is conscious of the Gift, the path is plain.

DEUS TERMINUS

DEUS TERMINUS

THE practical Roman, stern constructor of roads and codes, when he needs must worship, loved a deity practical as himself; and in his parcelling of the known world into plots, saying unto this man, Bide here, and to that, Sit you down there, he could scarce fail to evolve the god Terminus: visible witness of possession and dominion, type of solid facts not to be quibbled away. We Romans of this latter day — so hailed by others, or complacently christened by ourselves — are Roman in nothing more than in this; and, as much in the less tangible realms of thought as in our solid acres, we are fain to set up the statue which shall proclaim that so much country is explored, marked out, allotted, and done with; that such and such ramblings and excursions are practicable and permissible, and all else is exploded, illegal, or absurd. And in this way we are left with naught but a vague lingering tradition of the happier days before the advent of the ruthless deity.

The sylvan glories of yonder stretch of woodland renew themselves each autumn, regal as ever. It is only the old enchantment that is gone; banished by the matter-of-fact deity, who has stolidly settled exactly where Lord A.'s shooting ends and Squire B.'s begins. Once, no such petty limitations fettered the mind. A step into the woodland was a step over the border — the margin of the material; and then, good-bye to the modern world of the land-agent and the "Field" advertisement! A chiming of little bells over your head, and lo! the peregrine, with eyes like jewels, fluttered through the trees,

Deus Terminus

her jesses catching in the boughs. 'Twas the favourite of the Princess, the windows of whose father's castle already gleamed through the trees, where honours and favours awaited the adventurous. The white doe sprang away through the thicket, her snowy flank stained with blood; she made for the enchanted cot, and for entrance you too had the pass-word. Did you fail on her traces, nor fox nor mole was too busy to spare a moment for friendly advice or information. Little hands were stretched to trip you, fairy gibe and mockery pelted you from every rabbit-hole; and O what Dryads you have kissed among the leaves, in that brief blissful moment ere they hardened into tree! 'Tis pity, indeed, that this sort of thing should have been made to share the suspicion attaching to the poacher; that the stony stare of the boundary god should confront you at the end of every green ride and rabbit-run; while the very rabbits themselves are too disgusted with the altered circumstances to tarry a moment for so much as to exchange the time of day.

Truly this age is born, like Falstaff, with a white head and something a round belly: and will none of your jigs and fantasies. The golden era of princesses is past. For your really virtuous 'prentices there still remain a merchant's daughter or two, and a bottle of port o' Sundays on the Clapham mahogany. For the rest of us, one or two decent clubs, and plenty of nice roomy lunatic asylums. " Go spin, you jade, go spin ! " is the one greeting for Imagination. And yet — what a lip the slut has ! What an ankle ! Go to : there's nobody looking; let us lock the door, pull down the blinds, and write us a merry ballad.

'Tis ungracious, perhaps, to regret what

Deus Terminus

is gone for ever, when so much is given in
return. A humour we have, that is entirely
new; and allotments that shall win back
Astræa. Our Labor Program stands for
evidence that the Board School, at least,
has done enduring work; and the useless
race of poets is fast dying out. Though
we no longer conjecture what song the
Sirens sang, or what name Achilles as-
sumed when he hid himself among women,
yet many a prize (of guineas galore) awaits
the competitor who will stoop, week by
week, to more practical research. "Le
monde marche," as Renan hath it, "vers
une sorte d'americanisme. . . . Peut-être
la vulgarité générale sera-t-elle un jour la
condition du bonheur des élus. Nous
n'avons pas le droit d'etre fort difficiles."
We will be very facile, then, since needs
must; remembering the good old proverb
that "scornful dogs eat dirty puddings."
But, ere we show Terminus the door, at

least let us fling one stone at the shrieking
sulphureous houses of damnation erected
as temples in his honour, and dignified
with his name! There, 'mid clangour,
dirt, and pestilence of crowding humanity,
the very spirit of worry and unrest sits
embodied. The old Roman was not such
a bad fellow. His deity of demarcation
at least breathed open air, and knew the
kindly touch of sun and wind. His simple
rites were performed amid flowers and
under blue sky, by sunny roads or tranquil
waters; and on this particular altar the
sacrifice was ordained to be free from any
stain of gore. Our hour of sacrifice, alas,
has not yet come. When it does — (*et
haud procul absit !*) — let the offering be
no bloodless one, but let (for choice) a fat
and succulent stationmaster smoke and
crackle on the altar of expiation!

OF SMOKING

OF SMOKING

CONCERNING Cigarette Smoking:
It hath been well observed by a
certain philosopher that this is a practice
commendable enough, and pleasant to
indulge in, "when you're not smoking";
wherein the whole criticism of the cigarette
is found, in a little room. Of the same
manner of thinking was one that I knew,
who kept by him an ample case bulging
with cigarettes, to smoke while he was
filling his pipe. Toys they be verily, *nugæ*,
and shadows of the substance. Serviceable, nevertheless, as shadows sometimes
be when the substance is temporarily unattainable; as between the acts of a play,
in the park, or while dressing for dinner:
that such moments may not be entirely

wasted. That cigarette, however, which is so prompt to appear after dinner I would reprehend and ban and totally abolish: as enemy to that diviner thing before which it should pale its ineffectual fires in shame — to wit, good drink, " *la dive bouteille* " ; except indeed when the liquor be bad, as is sometimes known to happen. Then it may serve in some sort as a sorry consolation. But to leave these airy substitutes, and come to smoking.

It hath been ofttimes debated whether the morning pipe be the sweeter, or that first pipe of the evening which " Hesperus, who bringeth all good things," brings to the weary with home and rest. The first is smoked on a clearer palate, and comes to unjaded senses like the kiss of one's first love; but lacks that feeling of perfect fruition, of merit recompensed and the goal and the garland won, which clings to the vesper bowl. Whence it comes

Of Smoking

that the majority give the palm to the latter. To which I intend no slight when I find the incense that arises at matins sweeter even than that of evensong. For, although with most of us who are labourers in the vineyard, toilers and swinkers, the morning pipe is smoked in hurry and fear and a sense of alarums and excursions and fleeting trains, yet with all this there are certain halcyon periods sure to arrive — Sundays, holidays, and the like — the whole joy and peace of which are summed up in that one beatific pipe after breakfast, smoked in a careless majesty like that of the gods "when they lie beside their nectar, and the clouds are lightly curled." Then only can we be said really to smoke. And so this particular pipe of the day always carries with it festal reminiscences: memories of holidays past, hopes for holidays to come; a suggestion of sunny lawns and flannels and the ungirt loin; a sense withal of something free and stately, as of "faint march-music in the air," or the old Roman cry of "Liberty, freedom, and enfranchisement."

If there be any fly in the pipe-smoker's ointment, it may be said to lurk in the matter of "rings." Only the exceptionally gifted smoker can recline in his chair and emit at will the perfect smoke-ring, in consummate eddying succession. He of the meaner sort must be content if, at rare heaven-sent intervals — while thinking, perhaps, of nothing less — there escape from his lips the unpremeditated flawless circle. Then "*deus fio*" he is moved to cry, at that breathless moment when his creation hangs solid and complete, ere the particles break away and blend with the baser atmosphere. Nay, some will deny to any of us terrene smokers the gift of fullest achievement:

Of Smoking

for what saith *the* poet of the century?
" On the earth the broken arcs: in the
heaven the perfect round!"

It was well observed by a certain character in one of Wilkie Collins's novels (if
an imperfect memory serveth me rightly)
that women will take pleasure in scents
derived from animal emanations, clarified
fats, and the like; yet do illogically abhor
the " clean, dry, vegetable smell" of
tobacco. Herein the true base of the
feminine objection is reached; being, as
usual, inherent want of logic rather than
any distaste, in the absolute, for the thing
in question. Thinking that they ought
to dislike, they do painfully cast about for
reasons to justify their dislike, when none
really exist. As a specimen of their so-
called arguments, I remember how a certain fair one triumphantly pointed out to
me that my dog, though loving me well,
could yet never be brought to like the

smell of tobacco. To whom I, who re-spected my dog (as Ben saith of Master Shakespeare) on this side idolatry as much as anything, was yet fain to point out — more in sorrow than in anger — that a dog, being an animal who delights to pass his whole day, from early morn to dewy eve, in shoving his nose into every carrion beastliness that he can come across, could hardly be considered *arbiter elegantiarum* in the matter of smells. But indeed I did wrong to take such foolish quibbling seriously; nor would I have done so, if she hadn't dragged my poor innocent dog into the discussion.

Of Smoking in Bed: There be who consider this a depravity — an instance of that excess in the practice of a virtue which passes into vice — and couple it with dram-drinking: who yet fail to justify themselves by argument. For if bed be by common consent the greatest bliss,

Of Smoking

the divinest spot, on earth, "*ille terrarum qui præter omnes angulus ridet*" ; and if tobacco be the true Herb of Grace, and a joy and healing balm, and respite and nepenthe, — if all this be admitted, why are two things, super-excellent separately, noxious in conjunction? And is not the Bed-Smoker rather an epicure in pleasure — self-indulgent perhaps, but still the triumphant creator of a new "blend," reminding one of a certain traveller's account of an intoxicant patronised in the South Sea Islands, which combines the blissful effect of getting drunk and remaining sober to enjoy it? Yet I shall not insist too much on this point, but would only ask — so long as the smoker be unwedded — for some tolerance in the matter and a little logic in the discussion thereof.

Concerning Cigars: That there be large sums given for these is within common

knowledge.   1*d*., 2*d*., nay even 4*d*., is not
too great a price, if a man will have of the
finest leaf, reckless of expense.   In this
sort of smoking, however, I find more of
vainglory and ostentation than solid satisfaction; and its votaries would seem to
display less a calm, healthy affection for
tobacco than (as Sir T. Browne hath it)
a "passionate prodigality."   And, besides
grievous wasting of the pocket, atmos-
pheric changes, varyings in the crops, and
the like, cause uncertainty to cling about
each individual weed, so that man is
always more or less at the mercy of Nature
and the elements — an unsatisfactory and
undignified position in these latter days
of the Triumphant Democracy.   But worst
and fatallest of all, to every cigar-smoker
it is certain to happen that once in his
life, by some happy combination of time,
place, temperament, and Nature — by
some starry influence, maybe, or freak of

Of Smoking

the gods in mocking sport — once, and
once only, he will taste the aroma of the
perfect leaf at just the perfect point — the
ideal cigar. Henceforth his life is sad-
dened; as one kissed by a goddess in a
dream, he goes thereafter, as one might
say, in a sort of love-sickness. Seeking
he scarce knows what, his existence becomes a dissatisfied yearning; the world
is spoiled for him, its joys are tasteless:
so he wanders, vision-haunted, down dreary
days to some miserable end.

Yet, if one will walk this path and take
the risks, the thing may be done at com-
paratively small expense. To such I would
commend the Roman motto, slightly altered — *Alieni appetens, sui avarus.* There
be always good fellows, with good cigars
for their friends. Nay, too, the boxes of
these lie open; and the good cigar belongs
rather to him that can appreciate it aright
than to the capitalist who, owing to a false

social system, happens to be its temporary guardian and trustee. Again there is a saying — bred first, I think, among the schoolmen at Oxford — that it is the duty of a son to live up to his father's income. Should any young man have found this task too hard for him, after the most strenuous and single-minded efforts, at least he can resolutely smoke his father's cigars. In the path of duty complete success is not always to be looked for; but an approving conscience, the sure reward of honest endeavour, is within reach of all.

AN AUTUMN
ENCOUNTER

AN AUTUMN ENCOUNTER

FOR yet another mile or two the hot
dusty road runs through level fields,
till it reaches yonder shoulder of the
downs, already golden three-parts up with
ripening corn.   Thitherwards lies my inevitable way; and now that home is almost
in sight it seems hard that the last part
of the long day's sweltering and delight-
ful tramp must needs be haunted by that
hateful speck, black on the effulgence of
the slope.   Did I not know he was only a
scarecrow, the thing might be in a way
companionable: a pleasant suggestive surmise, piquing curiosity, gilding this last
weary stage with some magic of expec-
tancy.   But I passed close by him on my
way out.   Early as I was, he was already

up and doing, eager to introduce himself.
He leered after me as I swung down the
road, — mimicked my gait, as it seemed,
in a most uncalled-for way: and when I
looked back, he was blowing derisive
kisses of farewell with his empty sleeve.

I had succeeded, however, in shaking
off the recollection between the morning's
start and now; so it was annoying that
he should force himself on me, just when
there was no getting rid of him. At this
distance, however, he might be anything.
An indeterminate blot, it seems to waver,
to falter, to come and vanish again in the
quivering, heated air. Even so, in the
old time, leaning on that familiar gate —
are the tell-tale inwoven initials still
decipherable? — I used to watch Her pac-
ing demurely towards me through the
corn. It was ridiculous, it was fatuous,
under all the circumstances it was mon-
strous, and yet . . . ! We were both

An Autumn Encounter

under twenty, so She was She, and I was
I, and there were only we three the wide
world over, she and I and the unbetray-
ing gate. *Porta eburnea!* False visions
alone sped through you, though Cupid was
wont to light on your topmost bar, and
preen his glowing plumes. And to think
that I should see her once more, coming
down the path as if not a day had passed,
hesitating as of old, and then — but surely
her ankles seem —— Confound that scarecrow! . . .

His sex is by this time painfully evident; also his condition in life, which is
as of one looking back on better days.
And now he is upon a new tack. Though
here on the level it is still sultry and
airless, an evening breeze is playing
briskly along the slope where he stands,
and one sleeve saws the air violently; the
other is pointed stiffly heavenwards. It
is all plain enough, my poor friend! The

sins of the world are a heavy burden and a grievous unto you. You have a mission, you must testify; it will forth, in season and out of season. For man, he wakes and sleeps and sins betimes: but crows sin steadily, without any cessation. And this unhappy state of things is your own particular business. Even at this distance I seem to hear you rasping it: "Salvation, damnation, damnation, salvation!" And the jolly earth smiles in the perfect evenglow, and the corn ripples and laughs all round you, and one young rook (only fledged this year, too!), after an excellent simulation of prostrate, heartbroken penitence, soars joyously away, to make love to his neighbour's wife. "Salvation, damnation, damn ——" A shifty wriggle of the road, and he is transformed once more. Flung back in an ecstasy of laughter, holding his lean sides, his whole form writhes with the chuckle and gurgle

An Autumn Encounter

of merriment. Ho, ho! what a joke it was! How I took you all in! Even the rooks! What a joke is everything, to be sure!

Truly, I shall be glad to get quit of this heartless mummer. Fortunately I shall soon be past him. And now, behold! the old dog waxes amorous. Mincing, mowing, empty sleeve on hollow breast, he would fain pose as the most irresistible old hypocrite that ever paced a metropolitan kerb. "Love, you young dogs," he seems to croak, "Love is the one thing worth living for! Enjoy your present, rooks and all, as I do!" Why, indeed, should he alone be insensible to the golden influence of the hour? More than one supple waist (alas! for universal masculine frailty!) has been circled by that tattered sleeve in days gone by; a throbbing heart once beat where sodden straw now fails to give a manly curve to the chest.

Pagan Papers

Why should the coat survive, and not a particle of the passion that inspired it long ago?

At last I confront him, face to face: and the villain grins recognition, completely unabashed. Nay, he cocks his eye with a significant glance under the slouch of his shapeless hat, and his arm points persistently and with intelligence up the road. My good fellow, I know the way to the Dog and Duck as well as you do: I was going there anyhow, without your officious interference — and the beer, as you justly remark, is unimpeachable. But was this really all you 've been trying to say to me, this last half-hour? Well, well!

THE WHITE
POPPY

THE WHITE POPPY

A RIOT of scarlet on gold, the red poppy of our native fields tosses heavy tresses with gipsy *abandon;* her sister of the sea-shore is golden, a yellow blossom that loves the keen salt savour of the spray. Of another hue is the poppy of history, of romance, of the muse. White as the stark death-shroud, pallid as the cheeks of that queen of a silent land whose temples she languorously crowns, ghost-like beside her fuller-blooded kin, she droops dream-laden, *Papaver somniferum,* the poppy of the magic juice of oblivion. In the royal plenitude of summer, the scarlet blooms will sometimes seem but a red cry from earth in memory of the many dews of battle that have drenched

these acres in years gone by, for little end
but that these same "bubbles of blood"
might glow to-day; the yellow flower does
but hint of the gold that has dashed a
thousand wrecks at her feet around these
shores: for happier suggestion we must
turn to her of the pallid petals, our white
Lady of Consolation. Fitting hue to typ-
ify the crowning blessing of forgetfulness!
Too often the sable robes of night dis-
semble sleeplessness, remorse, regret, self-
questioning. Let black, then, rather stand
for hideous memory: white for blessed
blank oblivion, happiest gift of the gods!
For who, indeed, can say that the record
of his life is not crowded with failure and
mistake, stained with its petty cruelties
of youth, its meannesses and follies of
later years, all which storm and clamour
incessantly at the gates of memory, refus-
ing to be shut out? Leave us alone, O
gods, to remember our felicities, our suc-

The White Poppy

cesses: only aid us, ye who recall no gifts,
aptly and discreetly to forget.

Discreetly, we say; for it is a tactful
forgetfulness that makes for happiness.
In the minor matter, for instance, of
small money obligations, that shortness
of memory which the school of Professors
Panurge and Falstaff rashly praises, may
often betray into some unfortunate allusion or reference to the subject which
shall pain the delicate feelings of the
obliger; or, if he be of coarser clay, shall
lead him in his anger to express himself
with unseemliness, and thereby to do vio-
lence to his mental tranquillity, in which
alone, as Marcus Aurelius teacheth, lieth
the perfection of moral character. This
is to be a stumbling-block and an offence
against the brethren. It is better to keep
just memory enough to avoid such hidden
rocks and shoals; in which thing Mr.
Swiveller is our great exemplar, whose

mental map of London was a chart wherein every creditor was carefully "buoyed."

The wise man prays, we are told, for a
good digestion: let us add to the prayer
— and a bad memory. Truly we are
sometimes tempted to think that we are
the only ones cursed with this corroding
canker. Our friends, we can swear, have
all, without exception, atrocious memories; why is ours alone so hideously
vital? Yet this isolation must be imag-
inary; for even as we engage in this selfish
moan for help in our own petty case, we
are moved to add a word for certain others
who, meaning no ill, unthinkingly go
about to add to humanity's already heavy
load of suffering. How much needless
misery is caused in this world by the reckless "recollections" of dramatic and other
celebrities? You gods, in lending ear to
our prayer, remember too, above all other
sorts and conditions of men, these our

The White Poppy

poor erring brothers and sisters, the some-
time *sommités* of Mummerdom!

Moments there are, it is true, when this
traitor spirit tricks you: when some subtle
scent, some broken notes of an old song,
nay, even some touch of a fresher air on
your cheeks at night — a breath of "*le
vent qui vient à travers la montagne*" —
have power to ravish, to catch you back
to the blissful days when you trod the
one authentic Paradise. Moments only,
alas! Then the evil crowd rushes in
again, howls in the sacred grove, tramples
down and defiles the happy garden; and
once more you cry to Our Lady of Sleep,
crowned of the white poppy. And you
envy your dog who, for full discharge of
a present benefaction having wagged you
a hearty, expressive tail, will then pursue
it gently round the hearth-rug till, in
restful coil, he reaches it at last, and
oblivion with it; every one of his half-

dozen diurnal sleeps being in truth a royal amnesty.

But whose the hand that shall reach us the herb of healing? Perdita blesses every guest at the shearing with a handful of blossom; but this gift is not to be asked of her whose best wish to her friends is "grace and remembrance." The fair Ophelia, rather: nay, for as a nursling she hugs her grief, and for her the memory of the past is a "sorrow's crown of sorrow." What flowers are these her pale hand offers? "There's pansies, that's for thoughts!" For me rather, O dear Ophelia, the white poppy of forgetfulness!

A BOHEMIAN
IN EXILE

A BOHEMIAN IN EXILE

WHEN, many years ago now, the once potent and extensive kingdom of Bohemia gradually dissolved and passed away, not a few historians were found to chronicle its past glories; and some have gone on to tell the fate of this or that once powerful chieftain who either donned the swallow-tail and conformed or, proudly self-exiled, sought some quiet retreat and died as he had lived, a Bohemian. But these were of the princes of the land. To the people, the villeins, the common rank and file, does no interest attach? Did they waste and pine, anæmic, in thin, strange, unwonted air? Or sit at the table

131

of the scornful and learn, with Dante, how salt was alien bread? It is of one of those faithful commons I would speak, narrating only "the short and simple annals of the poor."

It is to be noted that the kingdom aforesaid was not so much a kingdom as a United States — a collection of self-ruling guilds, municipalities, or republics, bound together by a common method of viewing life. "There *once* was a king of Bohemia" — but that was a long time ago, and even Corporal Trim was not certain in whose reign it was. These small free States, then, broke up gradually, from various causes and with varying speed; and I think ours was one of the last to go.

With us, as with many others, it was a case of lost leaders. "Just for a handful of silver he left us"; though it was not exactly that, but rather that, having got the handful of silver, they wanted a wider hori-

A Bohemian in Exile

zon to fling it about under than Bloomsbury afforded.

> " So they left us for their pleasure; and in due time,
> one by one — "

But I will not be morose about them; they had honestly earned their success, and we all honestly rejoiced at it, and do so still.

When old Pan was dead and Apollo's bow broken, there were many faithful pagans who would worship at no new shrines, but went out to the hills and caves, truer to the old gods in their dis-crowned desolation than in their pomp and power. Even so were we left behind, a remnant of the faithful. We had never expected to become great in art or song; it was the life itself that we loved; that was our end — not, as with them, the means to an end.

> " We aimed at no glory, no lovers of glory we;
> Give us the glory of going on and still to be. "

Pagan Papers

Unfortunately, going on was no longer possible; the old order had changed, and we could only patch up our broken lives as best might be.

Fothergill said that he, for one, would have no more of it. The past was dead, and he wasn't going to try to revive it. Henceforth he, too, would be dead to Bloomsbury. Our forefathers, speaking of a man's death, said " he changed his life." This is how Fothergill changed his life and died to Bloomsbury. One morning he made his way to the Whitechapel Road, and there he bought a barrow. The Whitechapel barrows are of all sizes, from the barrow wheeled about by a boy with half a dozen heads of cabbages to barrows drawn by a tall pony, such as on Sundays take the members of a club to Epping Forest. They are all precisely the same in plan and construction, only in the larger sizes the handles develop or evolve

A Bohemian in Exile

into shafts; and they are equally suitable,
according to size, for the vending of
whelks, for a hot-potato can, a piano
organ, or for the conveyance of a cheery
and numerous party to the Derby. Fothergill bought a medium sized " developed "
one, and also a donkey to fit; he had it
painted white, picked out with green —
the barrow, not the donkey — and when
his arrangements were complete, stabled
the whole for the night in Bloomsbury.
The following morning, before the early
red had quite faded from the sky, the
exodus took place, those of us who were
left being assembled to drink a parting
whisky-and-milk in sad and solemn silence.
Fothergill turned down Oxford Street, sit-
ting on the shaft with a short clay in his
mouth, and disappeared from our sight,
heading west at a leisurely pace. So he
passed out of our lives by way of the
Bayswater Road.

Pagan Papers

They must have wandered far and seen many things, he and his donkey, from the fitful fragments of news that now and again reached us. It seems that eventually, his style of living being economical, he was enabled to put down his donkey and barrow, and set up a cart and a mare — no fashionable gipsy-cart, a sort of houseboat on wheels, but a light and serviceable cart, with a moveable tilt, constructed on his own designs. This allowed him to take along with him a few canvases and other artists' materials; soda-water, whisky, and such like necessaries; and even to ask a friend from town for a day or two, if he wanted to.

He was in this state of comparative luxury when at last, by the merest accident, I foregathered with him once more. I had pulled up to Streatley one afternoon, and, leaving my boat, had gone for a long ramble on the glorious North Berkshire

A Bohemian in Exile

Downs to stretch my legs before dinner. Somewhere over on Cuckhamsley Hill, by the side of the Ridgeway, remote from the habitable world, I found him, smoking his vesper pipe on the shaft of his cart, the mare cropping the short grass beside him. He greeted me without surprise or effusion, as if we had only parted yesterday, and without a hint of an allusion to past times, but drifted quietly into rambling talk of his last three years, and, without ever telling his story right out, left a strange picturesque impression of a nomadic life which struck one as separated by fifty years from modern conventional existence. The old road-life still lingered on in places, it seemed, once one got well away from the railway: there were two Englands existing together, the one fringing the great iron highways wherever they might go — the England under the eyes of most of us. The other, unguessed at by many, in whatever places were still vacant of shriek and rattle, drowsed on as of old: the England of heath and common and windy sheep down, of by-lanes and village-greens — the England of Parson Adams and Lavengro. The spell of the free untrammelled life came over me as I listened, till I was fain to accept of his hospitality and a horse-blanket for the night, oblivious of civilised comforts down at the Bull. On the downs where Alfred fought we lay and smoked, gazing up at the quiet stars that had shone on many a Dane lying stark and still a thousand years ago; and in the silence of the lone tract that enfolded us we seemed nearer to those old times than to these I had left that afternoon, in the now hushed and sleeping valley of the Thames.

When the news reached me, some time later, that Fothergill's aunt had died and left him her house near town and the

A Bohemian in Exile

little all she had possessed, I heard it
with misgivings, not to say forebodings.
For the house had been his grandfather's,
and he had spent much of his boyhood
there; it had been a dream of his early
days to possess it in some happy future,
and I knew he could never bear to sell
or let it. On the other hand, can you
stall the wild ass of the desert? And will
not the caged eagle mope and pine?

However, possession was entered into,
and all seemed to go well for the time.
The cart was honourably installed in
the coach-house, the mare turned out to
grass. Fothergill lived idly and happily,
to all seeming, with " a book of verses
underneath the bough," and a bottle of
old claret for the friend who might chance
to drop in. But as the year wore on small
signs began to appear that he who had
always " rather hear the lark sing than
the mouse squeak " was beginning to feel

himself caged, though his bars were gilded.

I was talking one day to his coachman (he now kept three men-servants), and he told me that of a Sunday morning when the household had gone to church and everything was quiet, Mr. Fothergill would go into the coach-house and light his pipe, and sit on the step of the brougham (he had a brougham now), and gaze at the old cart, and smoke and say nothing; and smoke and say nothing again. He didn't like it, the coachman confessed; and to me it seemed ominous.

One morning late in March, at the end of a long hard winter, I was wakened by a flood of sunshine. The early air came warm and soft through the open window; the first magic suggestion of spring was abroad, with its whispered hints of daffodils and budding hawthorns; and one's blood danced to imagined pipings of Pan

A Bohemian in Exile

from happy fields far distant. At once I thought of Fothergill, and, with a certain foreboding of ill, made my way down to Holly Lodge as soon as possible. It was with no surprise at all that I heard that the master was missing. In the very first of the morning, it seemed, or ever the earliest under-housemaid had begun to set man-traps on the stairs and along the passages, he must have quietly left the house. The servants were cheerful enough, nevertheless, and thought the master must only have " gone for a nice long walk," and so on, after the manner of their kind. Without a word I turned my steps to the coach-house. Sure enough, the old cart was missing; the mare was gone from the paddock. It was no good my saying anything; pursuit of this wild haunter of tracks and by-paths would have been futile indeed. So I kept my own counsel. Fothergill never returned to Holly Lodge, and has been more secret and evasive since his last flight, rarely venturing on old camping grounds near home, like to a bird scared by the fowler's gun.

Once indeed, since then, while engaged in pursuit of the shy quarry known as the Early Perp., late Dec., E. Eng., and the like, specimens of which I was tracking down in the west, I hit upon him by accident; hearing in an old village rumours concerning a strange man in a cart who neither carried samples nor pushed the brewing interest by other means than average personal consumption — tales already beginning to be distorted into material for the myth of the future. I found him friendly as ever, equally ready to spin his yarns. As the evening wore on, I ventured upon an allusion to past times and Holly Lodge; but his air of puzzled politeness convinced me that the whole

A Bohemian in Exile

thing had passed out of his mind, as a slight but disagreeable incident in the even tenor of his nomadic existence.

After all, his gains may have outbalanced his losses. Had he cared, he might, with his conversational gifts, have been a social success; certainly, I think, an artistic one. He had great powers, had any impulse been present to urge him to execution and achievement. But he was for none of these things. Contemplative, receptive, with a keen sense of certain sub-tones and side-aspects of life unseen by most, he doubtless chose wisely to enjoy life his own way, and to gather from the fleeting days what bliss they had to give, nor spend them in toiling for a harvest to be reaped when he was dust.

> Some for the glories of this life, and some
> Sigh for the Prophet's Paradise to come :
> Ah, take the cash and let the credit go,
> Nor heed the rumble of a distant drum.

JUSTIFIABLE
HOMICIDE

JUSTIFIABLE HOMICIDE

THIS is a remedial age, an age of keys for all manner of locks; so he cannot be said to ask too much who seeks for exact information as to how a young man ought, in justice to himself and to society, to deal with his relations. During his minority he has lain entirely at their mercy: has been their butt, their martyr, their drudge, their *corpus vile.* Possessing all the sinews of war, this stiff-necked tribe has consistently refused to "part": even for the provision of those luxuries so much more necessary than necessities. Its members have crammed their victim full of precepts, rules of conduct, moral maxims, and most miscellaneous counsel: all which he intuitively suspected at the time, and has ascertained by subsequent experience, to be utterly worthless. Now, when their hour has come, when the tocsin has sounded at last, and the Gaul is at the gate, they still appear to think that the old condition of things is to go on; unconscious, apparently, of atonement due, of retribution to be exacted, of wrongs to be avenged and of insults to be wiped away!

Over the north-west frontier, where the writ of the English Raj runs not, the artless Afghan is happy in a code that fully provides for relatives who neglect or misunderstand their obligations. An Afghan it was who found himself compelled to reprove an uncle with an unfortunate habit of squandering the family estate. An excellent relative, this uncle, in all other respects. As a liar, he had few equals; he robbed with taste and discre-

Justifiable Homicide

tion; and his murders were all imbued with true artistic feeling. He might have lived to a green old age of spotless respectability but for his one little failing. As it was, justice had to be done, *ruat cælum:* and so it came about that one day the nephew issued forth to correct him with a matchlock. The innocent old man was cultivating his paternal acres; so the nephew was able, unperceived, to get a steady sight on him. His finger was on the trigger, when suddenly there slipped into his mind the divine precept: "Allah is merciful!" He lowered his piece, and remained for a little plunged in thought; meanwhile the unconscious uncle hoed his paddy. Then with a happy smile he took aim once more, for there also occurred to him the precept equally divine: "But Allah is also just." With an easy conscience he let fly, and behold! there was an uncle the more in Paradise.

Pagan Papers

It was probably some little affair of a
similar quality that constrained a recruit
in a regiment stationed at Peshawur to
apply for leave of absence: in order to
attend to family matters of importance.
The Colonel knew it was small use refus-
ing the leave, as in that case his recruit
would promptly desert; so he could only
ask, how long was the transaction like to
take? It was told him, after considera-
tion, that, allowing for all possible difficulties and delays, a month would meet
the necessities of the case; and on that
understanding he allowed his man to
depart. At the end of the month he
reappeared on duty, a subdued but mellow
cheer shining through his wonted impas-
siveness. His Colonel ventured to in-
quire of him, in a general way, if the
business in question were satisfactorily
concluded. And he replied: "I got him
from behind a rock."

Justifiable Homicide

There are practical difficulties in the way of the adoption of such methods at home. We must be content to envy, without imitating, these free and happy sons of the hills. And yet a few of the old school are left us still: averse from change, mistrustful of progress, sticking steadily to the good old-fashioned dagger and bowl. I had a friend who disposed of a relative every spring. Uncles were his special line — (he had suffered much from their tribe, having been early left an orphan) — though he had dabbled in aunts, and in his hot youth, when he was getting his hand in, he had even dallied with a grand-parent or two. But it was in uncles he excelled. He possessed (at the beginning of his career) a large number of these connections, and pursuit of them, from the mere sordid point of view of £ s. d., proved lucrative. But he always protested (and I believed him)

that gain with him was a secondary con-
sideration. It would hardly be in the
public interest to disclose his *modus
operandi.* I shall only remark that he
was one of the first to realise the security
and immunity afforded the artist by the
conditions of modern London. Hence it
happened that he usually practised in
town, but spent his vacations at the
country houses of such relations as were
still spared him, where he was always the
life and soul of the place. Unfortunately
he is no longer with us, to assist in the
revision of this article: nor was it permitted me to soothe his last moments.
The presiding Sheriff was one of those
new-fangled officials who insist on the
exclusion of the public, and he declined
to admit me either in the capacity of a
personal connection or, though I tried my
hardest, as the representative of "The
National Observer." It only remains to

Justifiable Homicide

be said of my much-tried and still la-
mented friend, that he left few relatives
to mourn his untimely end.

But our reluctant feet must needs keep
step with the imperious march of Time,
and my poor friend's Art (as himself in
later years would sorrowfully admit) is
now almost as extinct as the glass-stain-
ing of old, or "Robbia's craft so apt and
strange"; while our thin-blooded youth,
too nice for the joyous old methods, are
content to find sweetest revenge in severely
dropping their relations. This is indeed
a most effective position: it exasperates,
while it is unassailable. And yet there
remains a higher course, a nobler task.
Not mere forgiveness: it is simple duty
to forgive — even one's guardians. No
young man of earnest aspirations will be
content to stop there. Nay: lead them
on, these lost ones, by the hand; conduct
them "generously and gently, and with

linking of the arm"; educate them,
eradicate their false ideals, dispel their
foolish prejudices; be to their faults a
little blind and to their virtues very kind :
in fine, realise that you have a mission —
that these wretches are not here for nothing. The task will seem hard at first;
but only those who have tried can know
how much may be done by assiduous and
kindly effort towards the chastening —
ay! the final redemption even! — of the
most hopeless and pig-headed of uncles.

THE FAIRY
WICKET

THE FAIRY WICKET

FROM digging in the sandy, over-triturated soil of times historical, all dotted with date and number and sign, how exquisite the relief in turning to the dear days outside history — yet not so very far off neither for us nurslings of the northern sun — when kindly beasts would loiter to give counsel by the wayside, and a fortunate encounter with one of the Good People was a surer path to Fortune and the Bride than the best-worn stool that ever proved step-ladder to aspiring youth. For then the Fairy Wicket stood everywhere ajar — everywhere and to each and all. "Open, open, green hill!" — you needed no more recondite sesame than that: and, whoever you were,

you might have a glimpse of the elfin
dancers in the hall that is litten within
by neither sun nor moon; or catch at the
white horse's bridle as the Fairy Prince
rode through. It has been closed now
this many a year (the fairies, always
strong in the field, are excellent wicket-
keepers); and if it open at all, 'tis but for
a moment's mockery of the material generation that so deliberately turned its back
on the gap into Elf-Land — that first stage
to the Beyond.

It was a wanton trick, though, that
these folk of malice used to play on a
small school-boy, new kicked out of his
nest into the draughty, uncomfortable
outer world, his unfledged skin still craving the feathers whereinto he was wont to
nestle. The barrack-like school, the arid,
cheerless class-rooms, drove him to Nature
for redress; and, under an alien sky, he
would go forth and wander along the iron

The Fairy Wicket

road by impassive fields, so like yet so
unlike those hitherto a part of him and
responding to his every mood. And to
him, thus loitering with overladen heart,
there would come suddenly a touch of
warmth, of strange surprise. The turn of
the road just ahead — that, sure, is not all
unfamiliar? That row of elms — it cannot entirely be accident that they range
just *so?* And, if not accident, then round
the bend will come the old duck-pond,
the shoulder of the barn will top it, a few
yards on will be the gate — it swings-to
with its familiar click — the dogs race
down the avenue — and then — and then!
It is all wildly fanciful; and yet, though
knowing not Tertullian, a "*credo quia
impossibile*" is on his tongue as he quickens
his pace — for what else can he do? A
step, and the spell is shattered — all is
cruel and alien once more; while every
copse and hedge-row seems a-tinkle with

faint elfish laughter. The Fairies have had their joke: they have opened the wicket one of their own hand's-breadths, and shut it in their victim's face. When next that victim catches a fairy, he purposes to tie up the brat in sight of his own green hill, and set him to draw up a practical scheme for Village Councils.

One of the many women I ever really loved, fair in the fearless old fashion, was used to sing, in the blithe, unfettered accent of the people: "I'd like to be a fairy, And dance upon my toes, I'd like to be a fairy, And wear short close!" And in later life it is to her sex that the wee (but very wise) folk sometimes delegate their power of torment. Such understudies are found to play the part exceeding well; and many a time the infatuated youth believes he sees in the depth of one sole pair of eyes — blue, brown, or green (the fairy colour) — the authentic fairy

The Fairy Wicket

wicket standing ajar: many a time must
he hear the quaint old formula, "I'm
sure, if I've ever done anything to lead
you to think," etc. (runs it not so?), ere
he shall realise that here is the gate upon
no magic pleasance but on a cheap sub-
urban villa, banging behind the wrathful
rate-collector or hurled open to speed the
pallid householder to the Registrar's
Office. In still grosser habitations, too,
they lurk, do the People of Mischief,
ready to frolic out on the unsuspecting
one: as in the case, which still haunts
my memory, of a certain bottle of an
historic Château-Yquem, hued like Vene-
tian glass, odorous as a garden in June.
Forth from out the faint perfume of this
haunted drink there danced a bevy from
Old France, clad in the fashion of Louis-
Quinze, peach-coloured knots of ribbon
bedizening apple-green velvets, as they
moved in stately wise among the roses of

the old garden, to the quaint music —
Rameau, was it? — of a fairy *cornemuse*,
while fairy Watteaus, Fragonards, Lan-
crets, sat and painted them. Alas! too
shallow the bottle, too brief the brawls:
not to be recalled by any quantity of
Green Chartreuse.

ABOARD THE GALLEY

ABOARD THE GALLEY

HE was cruising in the Southern Seas (was the Ulysses who told me this tale), when there bore down upon him a marvellous strange fleet, whose like he had not before seen. For each little craft was a corpse, stiffly "marlined," or bound about with tarred rope, as mariners do use to treat plug tobacco: also ballasted, and with a fair mast and sail stepped through his midriff. These self-sufficing ships knew no divided authority: no pilot ever took the helm from the captain's hands; no mutines lay in bilboes, no passengers complained of the provisions. In a certain island to windward (the native pilot explained) it was the practice, when a man died, to bury him for the time

being in dry, desiccating sand, till a chief
should pass from his people, when the
waiting bodies were brought out and,
caulked and rigged *secumdum artem*, were
launched with the first fair breeze, the
admiral at their head, on their voyage to
the Blessed Islands. And if a chief
should die, and the sand should hold no
store of corpses for his escort, this simple
practical folk would solve the little diffi-
culty by knocking some dozen or twenty
stout fellows on the head, that the notable
might voyage like a gentleman. Whence
this gallant little company, running before
the breeze, stark, happy, and extinct, all
bound for the Isles of Light! 'Twas a
sight to shame us sitters at home, who
believe in those Islands, most of us, even
as they, yet are content to trundle City-
wards or to Margate, so long as the sorry
breath is in us; and, breathless at last, to
Bow or Kensal Green; without one effort,

dead or alive, to reach the far-shining Hesperides.

"Dans la galère capitane nous étions quatre-vingt rameurs!" sang the oarsmen in the ballad; and they, though indeed they toiled on the galley-bench, were free and happy pirates, members of an honoured and liberal profession. But all we — pirates, parsons, stockbrokers, whatever our calling — are but galley-slaves of the basest sort, fettered to the oar each for his little spell. A common misery links us all, like the chain that runs the length of the thwarts. Can *nothing* make it worth our while not to quarrel with our fellows? The menace of the storms is for each one and for all: the master's whip has a fine impartiality. Crack! the lash that scored my comrade's back has flicked my withers too; yet neither of us was shirking — it was that grinning ruffian in front. Well: to-morrow, God willing, the evasion shall be ours, while he writhes howling. But why do we never once combine — seize on the ship, fling our masters into the sea, and steer for some pleasant isle far down under the Line, beyond the still-vexed Bermoothes? When ho for feasting! Hey for tobacco and free-quarters! But no: the days pass, and are reckoned up, and done with; and ever more pressing cares engage. Those fellows on the leeward benches are having an easier time than we poor dogs on the weather side? Then, let us abuse, pelt, vilify them: let us steal their grub, and have at them generally for a set of shirking, malingering brutes! What matter that to-morrow they may be to windward, we to lee? We never can look ahead. And they know this well, the gods our masters, pliers of the whip And mayhap we like them none the worse for it.

Aboard the Galley

Indeed, there is a traitor sort among ourselves, that spins facile phrases in the honour of these whipmasters of ours — as "*omnes eodem cogimur,*" and the rest; which is all very pretty and mighty consoling. The fact is, the poets are the only people who score by the present arrangement; which it is therefore their interest to maintain. While we are doing all the work, these incorrigible skulkers lounge about and make ribald remarks; they write Greek tragedies on Fate, on the sublimity of Suffering, on the Petty Span, and so on; and act in a generally offensive way. And we are even weak enough to buy their books; offer them drinks, peerages, and things; and say what superlative fellows they are! But when the long-looked-for combination comes, and we poor devils have risen and abolished fate, destiny, the Olympian Council, early baldness, and the

like, these poets will really have to
go.

And when every rhymester has walked
the plank, shall we still put up with our
relations? True members of the "stupid
party," who never believe in us, who know
(and never forget) the follies of our
adolescence; who are always wanting us
not to do things; who are lavish of advice,
yet angered by the faintest suggestion of
a small advance in cash: shall the idle
singers perish and these endure? No: as
soon as the last poet has splashed over the
side, to the sharks with our relations!

The old barkey is lightening famously:
who shall be next to go? The Sportsman
of intolerable yarns: who slays twice
over — first, his game, and then the miserable being he button-holes for the tedious
recital. Shall we suffer *him* longer?
Who else? Who is that cowering under
the bulwarks yonder? The man who

Aboard the Galley

thinks he can imitate the Scottish accent!
Splash! And the next one? What a
crowd is here! How they block the
hatchways, lumber the deck, and get
between you and the purser's room —
these fadmongers, teetotallers, mission-
aries of divers isms! Overboard with
them, and hey for the Fortunate Isles!
Then for tobacco in a hammock 'twixt the
palms! Then for wine cooled in a brook-
let losing itself in silver sands! Then
for — but O these bilboes on our ankles,
how mercilessly they grip! The vertical
sun blisters the bare back: faint echoes
of Olympian laughter seem to flicker like
Northern Lights across the stark and
pitiless sky. One earnest effort would
do it, my brothers! A little modesty, a
short sinking of private differences; and
then we should all be free and equal
gentlemen of fortune, and I would be your
Captain! "Who? you? you would make

a pretty Captain!" Better than you,
you scurvy, skulking, little galley-slave!
"Galley-slave yourself, and be —— Pull
together, boys, and lie low! Here's the
Master coming with his whip!"

THE LOST
CENTAUR

THE LOST CENTAUR

IT is somewhere set down (or does the legend only exist in the great volume of ought-to-be-writ?) that the young Achilles, nurtured from babyhood by the wise and kindly Cheiron, accustomed to reverence an ideal of human skill and wisdom blent with all that was best and noblest of animal instinct, strength and swiftness, found poor humanity sadly to miss, when at last he was sent forth among his pottering little two-legged peers. Himself alone he had hitherto fancied to be the maimed one, the incomplete; he looked to find the lords of earth even such as these Centaurs; wise and magnanimous atop: below, shod with the lightning, winged with the wind, terrible

in the potentiality of the armed heel.
Instead of which——! How fallen was
his first fair hope of the world! And
even when reconciled at last to the dynasty
of the forked radish, after he had seen
its quality tested round the clangorous
walls of Troy—some touch of an im-
perial disdain ever lingered in his mind
for these feeble folk who could content-
edly hail him—him, who had known
Cheiron!—as hero and lord!

Achilles has passed, with the Centaurs
and Troy; but the feeling lingers.

Of strange and divers strands is twisted
the mysterious cord that, reaching back
" through spaces out of space and time-
less time," somewhere joins us to the
Brute; a twine of mingled yarn, not utterly base. As we grow from our animal
infancy, and the threads snap one by one
at each gallant wing-stroke of a soul pois-
ing for flight into Empyrean, we are yet

176

conscious of a loss for every gain, we have some forlorn sense of a vanished heritage. Willing enough are we to "let the ape and tiger die"; but the pleasant cousins dissembled in hide and fur and feather are not all tigers and apes: which last vile folk, indeed, exist for us only in picture-books, and chiefly offend by always carrying the Sunday School ensign of a Moral at their tails. Others — happily of less didactic dispositions — there be; and it is to these unaffected, careless companions that the sensible child is wont to devote himself; leaving severely alone the stiff, tame creatures claiming to be of closer kin. And yet these playmates, while cheerfully admitting him of their fellowship, make him feel his inferiority at every point. Vainly, his snub nose projected earthwards, he essays to sniff it with the terrier who (as becomes the nobler animal) is leading in the chase;

and he is ready to weep as he realises his loss. And the rest of the Free Company, — the pony, the cows, the great cart-horses, — are ever shaming him by their unboastful exercise of some enviable and unattainable attribute. Even the friendly pig, who (did but parents permit) should eat of his bread and drink of his cup, and be unto him as a brother, — which among all these unhappy bifurcations, so cheery, so unambitious, so purely contented, so apt to be the guide, philosopher, and friend of boyhood as he? What wonder that at times, when the neophyte in life begins to realise that all these desirable accomplishments have had to be surrendered one by one in the process of developing a Mind, the course of fitting out a Lord of Creation, he is wont — not knowing the extent of the kingdom to which he is heir — to feel a little discontented?

178

The Lost Centaur

Ere now this ill-humour, taking root in a nature wherein the animal is already ascendant, has led by downward paths to the Goat-Foot, in whom the submerged human system peeps out but fitfully, at exalted moments. He, the peevish and irascible, shy of trodden ways and pretty domesticities, is linked to us by little but his love of melody; but for which saving grace, the hair would soon creep up from thigh to horn of him. At times he will still do us a friendly turn: will lend a helping hand to poor little Psyche, wilfully seeking her own salvation; will stand shoulder to shoulder with us on Marathon plain. But in the main his sympathies are first for the beast: to which his horns are never horrific, but, with his hairy pelt, ever natural and familiar, and his voice (with its talk of help and healing) not harsh nor dissonant, but voice of very brother as well as very god.

Pagan Papers

And this declension — for declension it is, though we achieve all the confidences of Melampus, and even master with him the pleasant *argot* of the woods — may still be ours if we suffer what lives in us of our primal cousins to draw us down. On the other hand, let soul inform and irradiate body as it may, the threads are utterly shorn asunder never: nor is man, the complete, the self-contained, permitted to cut himself wholly adrift from these his poor relations. The mute and stunted human embryo that gazes appealingly from out the depths of their eyes must ever remind him of a kinship once (possibly) closer. Nay, at times, it must even seem to whelm him in reproach. As thus: " Was it really necessary, after all, that we two should part company so early? May you not have taken a wrong turning somewhere, in your long race after your so-called progress, after the perfection of

The Lost Centaur

this be-lauded species of yours? A turning whose due avoidance might perhaps
have resulted in no such lamentable cleav-
age as is here, but in some perfect em-
bodiment of the dual nature: as who
should say a being with the nobilities of
both of us, the basenesses of neither?
So might you, more fortunately guided,
have been led at last up the green sides
of Pelion, to the ancestral, the primeval,
Centaur still waiting majestic on the sum-
mit!" It is even so. Perhaps this thing
might once have been, O cousin outcast
and estranged! But the opportunity was
long since lost. Henceforth, two ways
for us for ever!

ORION

ORION

THE moonless night has a touch of frost, and is steely-clear. High and dominant amidst the Populations of the Sky, the restless and the steadfast alike, hangs the great Plough, lit with a hard radiance as of the polished and shining share. And yonder, low on the horizon, but half resurgent as yet, crouches the magnificent Hunter: watchful, seemingly, and expectant: with some hint of menace in his port.

Yet should his game be up, you would think, by now. Many a century has passed since the plough first sped a conqueror east and west, clearing forest and draining fen; policing the valleys with barbed-wires and Sunday schools, with the chains that are forged of peace, the irking fetters of plenty: driving also the whole lot of us, these to sweat at its tail, those to plod with the patient team, but all to march in a great chain-gang, the convicts of peace and order and law: while the happy nomad, with his woodlands, his wild cattle, his pleasing nuptialities, has long since disappeared, dropping only in his flight some store of flint-heads, a legacy of confusion. Truly, we Children of the Plough,. but for yon tremendous Monitor in the sky, were in right case to forget that the Hunter is still a quantity to reckon withal. Where, then, does he hide, the Shaker of the Spear? Why, here, my brother, and here; deep in the breasts of each and all of us! And for this drop of primal quicksilver in the blood what poppy or mandragora shall purge it hence away?

Of pulpiteers and parents it is called Original Sin: a term wherewith they brand whatever frisks and butts with rude goatish horns against accepted maxims and trim theories of education. In the abstract, of course, this fitful stirring of the old yeast is no more sin than a natural craving for a seat on a high stool, for the inscription — now horizontal, and now vertical — of figures, is sin. But the desk-men command a temporary majority: for the short while they shall hold the cards they have the right to call the game. And so — since we must bow to the storm — let the one thing be labelled Sin, and the other Salvation — for a season: ourselves forgetting never that it is all a matter of nomenclature. What we have now first to note is that this original Waft from the Garden asserts itself most vigorously in the Child. This it is that thrusts the small boy out under the naked heavens, to enact a sorry and shivering Crusoe on an islet in the duck-pond. This it is that sends the little girl footing it after the

gipsy's van, oblivious of lessons, puddings, the embrace maternal, the paternal
smack; hearing naught save the faint, far
bugle-summons to the pre-historic little
savage that thrills and answers in the ting-
ling blood of her; seeing only a troop of
dusky, dull-eyed guides along that shining highway to the dim land east o' the
sun and west o' the moon: where freedom
is, and you can wander and breathe, and
at night tame street lamps there are none
— only the hunter's fires, and the eyes of
lions, and the mysterious stars. In later
years it is stifled and gagged — buried
deep, a green turf at the head of it, and
on its heart a stone; but it lives, it
breathes, it lurks, it will up and out when
'tis looked for least. That stockbroker,
some brief summers gone, who was missed
from his wonted place one settling-day! a
goodly portly man, i' faith: and had a
villa and a steam launch at Surbiton: and

Orion

was versed in the esoteric humours of the
House. Who could have thought that the
Hunter lay hid in him? Yet, after many
weeks, they found him in a wild nook of
Hampshire. Ragged, sun-burnt, the noc-
turnal haystack calling aloud from his
frayed and weather-stained duds, his trou-
sers tucked, he was tickling trout with
godless native urchins; and when they
would have won him to himself with
honied whispers of American Rails, he
answered but with babble of green fields.
He is back in his wonted corner now:
quite cured, apparently, and tractable.
And yet — let the sun shine too wantonly
in Throgmorton Street, let an errant
zephyr, quick with the warm south, fan
but his cheek too wooingly on his way to
the station; and will he not once more
snap his chain and away? Ay, truly: and
next time he will not be caught.

Deans have danced to the same wild

piping, though their chapters have hushed
the matter up. Even Duchesses (they
say) have "come tripping doon the stair,"
rapt by the climbing passion from their
strawberry-leaved surroundings into star-
lit spaces. Nay, ourselves, too — the
douce, respectable mediocrities that we
are — which of us but might recall some
fearful outbreak whose details are merci-
fully unknown to the household that calls
us breadwinner and chief? What marvel
that up yonder the Hunter smiles? When
he knows that every one in his ken, the
tinker with the statesman, has caught his
bugle blast and gone forth on its irresistible appeal!

Not that they are so easily followed as
of yore, those flying echoes of the horn!
Joints are stiffer, maybe; certainly the
desolate suburbs creep ever farther into
the retreating fields; and when you reach
the windy moorland, lo! it is all staked

out into building-lots. Mud is muddier now than heretofore; and ruts are ruttier. And what friendless old beast comes limping down the dreary lane? He seems sorely shrunk and shoulder-shotten; but by the something of divinity in his look, still more than by the wings despondent along his mighty sides, 'tis ever the old Pegasus — not yet the knacker's own. "Hard times I've been having," he murmurs, as you rub his nose. "These fellows have really no seat except for a park hack. As for this laurel, we were wont to await it trembling: and in taking it we were afraid. Your English way of hunting it down with yelpings and hallooings — well, I may be out of date, but we wouldn't have stood that sort of thing on Helicon." So he hobbles down the road. Good-night, old fellow! Out of date? Well, it may be so. And alas! the blame is ours.

Pagan Papers

But for the Hunter — there he rises — couchant no more. Nay, flung full stretch on the blue, he blazes, he dominates, he appals! Will his turn, then, really come at last? After some Armageddon of cataclysmal ruin, all levelling, whelming the County Councillor with the Music-hall artiste, obliterating the very furrows of the Plough, shall the skin-clad nomad string his bow once more, and once more loose the whistling shaft? Wildly incredible it seems. And yet — look up! Look up and behold him confident, erect, majestic — there on the threshold of the sky!